THE HISTORY DETECTIVE INVESTIGATES

Roman Britain

Peter Hepplewhite

WAYLAND

The History Detective Investigates series:
Ancient Egypt
Ancient Greece
Ancient Sumer
Anglo-Saxons
Benin 900-1897 CE
Castles
The Celts
The Civil Wars
Early Islamic Civilization
The Indus Valley
The Industrial Revolution
Local History
Mayan Civilization
Monarchs
The Normans and the Battle of Hastings
Post-War Britain
Roman Britain
The Shang Dynasty of Ancient China
Stone Age to Iron Age
Tudor Exploration
Tudor Home
Tudor Medicine
Tudor Theatre
Tudor War
Victorian Crime
Victorian Factory
Victorian School
Victorian Transport
The Vikings
Weapons and Armour Through the Ages

Published in 2014 by Wayland
© Wayland 2014

Wayland
338 Euston Rd
London
NW1 3BH

Wayland Australia
Level 17/207 Kent Street
Sydney
NSW 2000

Editor: Hayley Leach
Designer: Simon Borrough
Cartoon artwork: Richard Hook
Maps and diagrams: Peter Bull

British Library Cataloguing in Publication Data
Roman Britain. - (The history detective investigates)
1. Romans - Great Britain - Social life and customs - Juvenile literature 2. Great Britain - History - Roman period, 55 B.C. - 449 A.D. - Juvenile literature
I. Title
936.1'04

ISBN 978 0 7502 8582 7

Printed in China

10 9 8 7 6 5 4 3

The publishers would like to thank the following for permission to reproduce their pictures:
akg-images/Erich Lessing 14, 16, 20; The Art Archive/Museo Capitolino Rome/Dagli Orti 4; Butser Ancient Farm 18 and 19; Dorset County Museum, UK/Bridgeman Art Library 20; R. Embleton 17; Robert Estall/Corbis 13; Jason Hawkes/Corbis 25; Museum of Antiquities, Newcastle 23; TopFoto.co.uk/Collection Roger-Viollet 5; TopFoto.co.uk cover, 7, 12 and title page, 16, 21, 26, 29, 28; TopFoto.co.uk/The British Museum 24, 25, 27 (bottom); Wayland Picture Library/Jim Kershaw 22 (left); The British Museum 22 (right).

Wayland is a division of Hachette Children's Books, an Hachette UK Company.
www.hachette.co.uk

First published in 2006 by Wayland

Contents

Words in **bold** can be found in the glossary on page 30

The history detective Sherlock Bones, will help you to find clues and collect evidence about Roman Britain. Wherever you see one of Sherlock's paw-prints, you will find a mystery to solve. The answers can be found on page 31.

1. Who were the Romans?

When the Romans invaded in AD 43 British tribes had little chance of defending their land against them. Roman armies were highly trained, well led and hardly ever lost a battle. Britain was about to become part of the mighty Roman Empire – whether the British liked it or not. Yet, the Romans had not always been so powerful. Their climb to greatness took many centuries.

The early Romans were farmers who lived on seven hills in a region called Latium, in what is now Italy. Little is known about their early history but, according to legend, the city of Rome was founded in 753 BC. At first the Romans only ruled the area around Rome but by 270 BC they had defeated neighbouring tribes and taken over the whole of Italy. And this was just the beginning! By AD 130 Roman armies had **conquered** most of Europe, North Africa and the Middle East.

As the Empire grew, so did Rome: from a small town into a vast capital city. At its peak the population reached almost one million, a huge number for the time. Taxes collected from conquered peoples made Rome rich. Triumphant generals built temples and arches to celebrate their victories, while the city centre boasted many grand buildings and monuments. Shops were filled with luxury goods from across the Roman world such as gold from Spain, honey from Greece and papyrus from Egypt.

How did Rome get its name? The Legend of Romulus and Remus

The god of war, Mars, had twin baby sons called Romulus and Remus. They were left to drown in a basket on the banks of the River Tiber but a she-wolf rescued them and fed them on her milk. Later, a shepherd stumbled across the boys and brought them up as his own sons. When the twins grew into strong men they built a city on the spot where the wolf had rescued them. Sadly, they couldn't agree who would be king and quarrelled. Romulus killed his brother and called the new city after himself – Rome.

Livy, a famous Roman historian (c. 59 BC – AD 17), retold the legend of Romulus and Remus in his book *The Early History of Rome.*

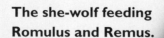

The she-wolf feeding Romulus and Remus.

This map shows the Roman Empire around the year 130 BC.
Everyone in the Roman Empire was governed by Roman laws.

A model of Ancient Rome. Can you see the race-track to the
left of this picture? It was used for chariot races.

✿ The large round building in the photograph is called the
Colosseum. It was built by the **Emperor** Vespasian and his sons,
and opened in AD 80. What do you think it was used for?

DETECTIVE WORK
The map on this page
shows the Roman names
for the countries inside
the Empire. Use an atlas
to find the modern names
of the countries the
Romans once ruled.

2. What was Celtic Britain like before the Romans?

Caledonii
Venicones
Damnonii
Votadini
Selgovae
Novantae
Corvetii
Brigantes
Parisi
Deceangli
Ordovices
Cornovii
Coritani
Demetae
Dobunni
Iceni
Silures
Catuvellauni
Atribates
Trinovantes
Belgae
Cantiaci
Dumnonii
Durotriges
Regnenses

This map shows where the different Celtic tribes lived. The Romans were able to bribe some of the tribes to help them when they invaded.

When the Romans invaded Britain the native people were called **Celts**. Celts also lived in the countries we now know as France, Belgium and Switzerland. British Celts lived in different tribes such as the **Iceni** in East Anglia or the Dumnonii in the West Country. Each tribe had its own ruler. Usually this was a king but under Celtic law a woman could become queen. In AD **60**, for example, the Brigantes, a tribe in the north of England, were led by Queen Cartimandua.

The Romans fought against Celtic peoples for over 500 years and thought they were barbarians. Roman historians described them as 'blue painted with only one redeeming feature – bravery'. Modern **archaeologists** have found evidence such as the presence of fine Celtic jewellery to show that the Celts were not **barbarians** and that in some things, like farming, they were more skilled than the Romans.

DETECTIVE WORK

Find where you live on the map. Which tribe would you have belonged to? Find out if there are any places near you with Celtic names like the river Avon, the Pennine mountains or the City of London. *The Oxford Dictionary of Place Names* is a great place to start.

Celtic men wore trousers, a short linen tunic and a long woollen cloak. Women wore tight-waisted bell shaped skirts. Shoes were made of leather or linen.

The Celts lived in round huts with walls made from wattle (woven branches) and daub (clay and mud cement). Celtic farmers were the first in Britain to protect the fertility of the fields. They sowed their crops and spread them with manure each year, instead of clearing new land when the soil was exhausted. Even the Romans admitted the Celts had better ploughs, sturdily built, with iron blades to turn heavy soils. Their diet was good too and included plenty of meat and fish. A favourite Celtic dish was salmon baked with honey and herbs.

Celtic craftsmen were highly skilled. Their metal workers made iron weapons like helmets and long swords but also decorative jewellery such as gold and silver torcs, or neck rings. Spinners, weavers and dyers, often women, made clothes of such quality and colour, that British woollen cloaks became famous across the Roman world. Celtic boat builders were so good that the Romans used the skills of the Celtic people they had already **conquered** in **Gaul** to build the transport for the fleets that invaded Britain.

🐾 Look at the photograph of Maiden Castle built by the Durotriges tribe. How many sets of walls does it have? Why do you think they built so many?

Celtic tribes were warlike and often fought against each other. To defend themselves they built hill-forts with massive earth banks topped with walls or wooden stakes. This hill-fort in Dorset is called Maiden Castle.

3. Why did the Romans invade Britain?

The Celts were brave warriors and skilled charioteers. They looked terrifying and often fought without armour, their bodies painted with dye. Celtic armies fought like mobs and it was hard for their leaders to give them orders when a battle had begun.

❀ Why do you think Caesar wrote about the great difficulties his troops faced when he raided Britain?

Julius **Caesar** was an ambitious general and politician who was scheming to rule Rome. In 55 BC, Caesar raided Britain with an army of two **legions**. He had recently beaten the Celts in **Gaul** and was angry that the British had been helping their kinsmen to fight him. But he had other motives too. He wanted to make his name so he could become the most powerful politician in Rome.

Caesar's Raid, 55 BC:

*The Romans opened fire from their ships with bows, slings and catapults. The natives backed off a little, but still the soldiers hesitated. Then the **Standard Bearer** of the Tenth **Legion** took action. He prayed to the gods for luck and cried out in a loud voice, 'Jump down comrades, unless you want to lose the Eagle to the enemy'. Ignoring the danger he leaped into the sea towards the British. Instantly the soldiers sprang after him. They could not face the shame of losing a Roman Eagle.*

Julius Caesar wrote this account in his autobiography, *The Conquest of Gaul*, only a few years after the attack on Britain took place. The eagle was the sacred symbol of the legion.

Caesar's invasion was almost a disaster. The British were waiting on the landing beaches and at first his troops were afraid to leave their boats. After a bloody battle, the Romans won but Caesar had to return to Gaul after a storm wrecked his ships. The next year, 54 BC, he tried again with a fleet of 800 ships and nearly 40,000 soldiers. This time he defeated the Celtic war leader Cassivellaunus and left with **hostages** and plunder.

It was almost 90 years before the Romans came back to Britain. In AD 43, Rome had a new **Emperor**, Claudius, who needed to prove himself to his generals, or risk being overthrown. The conquest of Britain, he decided, was the perfect way to be seen as a great leader. Conveniently, the British had already given him an excuse to attack. The tribes of southern Britain had been fighting among themselves: King Verica, an **ally** of Rome, had been driven from his kingdom. Verica, who ruled part of Sussex, appealed to Claudius for help. The Emperor was eager to send General Aulus Plautius and an army of 40,000 men to Verica's aid.

A set of Iron Age coins, including a silver coin of the Iceni tribe in the top row. As well as wanting to prove himself to his generals, Claudius had another reason to invade. He believed coins like these proved Britain was an island rich with silver mines and pearls.

DETECTIVE WORK

Use the Internet to find out about Claudius. What disabilities did he have and how did they make life harder for him?

Roman soldiers were highly trained and well organised. They were divided into legions of about 5,500 legionaries. A legionary could march 30 miles a day while carrying all his kit. This included a pickaxe, saw, bucket, cooking pots and food – as well as weapons and armour.

4. Who were Caratacus and Boudicca?

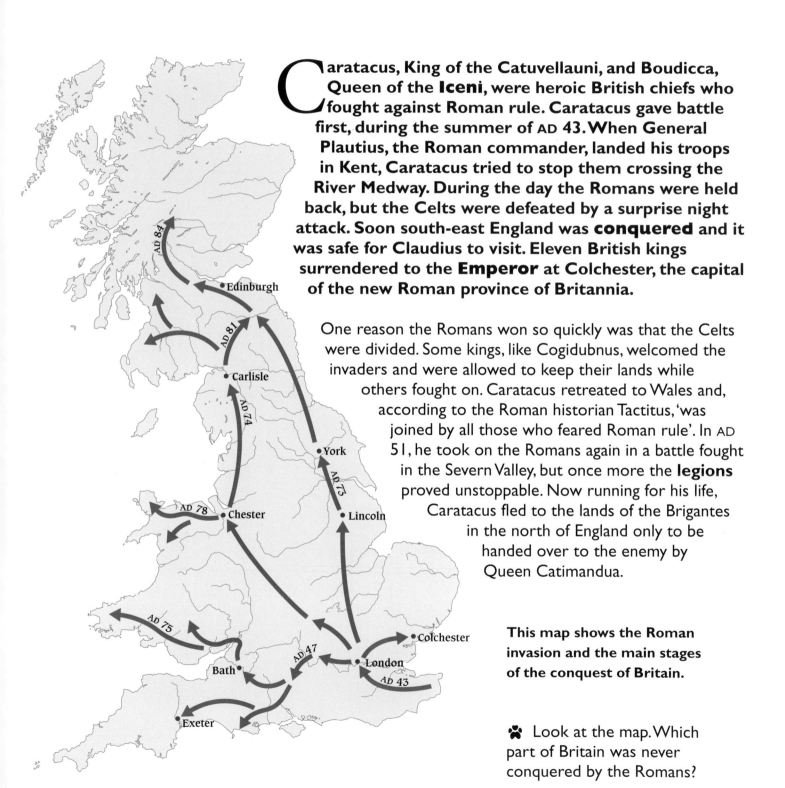

Caratacus, King of the Catuvellauni, and Boudicca, Queen of the **Iceni**, were heroic British chiefs who fought against Roman rule. Caratacus gave battle first, during the summer of AD 43. When General Plautius, the Roman commander, landed his troops in Kent, Caratacus tried to stop them crossing the River Medway. During the day the Romans were held back, but the Celts were defeated by a surprise night attack. Soon south-east England was **conquered** and it was safe for Claudius to visit. Eleven British kings surrendered to the **Emperor** at Colchester, the capital of the new Roman province of Britannia.

One reason the Romans won so quickly was that the Celts were divided. Some kings, like Cogidubnus, welcomed the invaders and were allowed to keep their lands while others fought on. Caratacus retreated to Wales and, according to the Roman historian Tactitus, 'was joined by all those who feared Roman rule'. In AD 51, he took on the Romans again in a battle fought in the Severn Valley, but once more the **legions** proved unstoppable. Now running for his life, Caratacus fled to the lands of the Brigantes in the north of England only to be handed over to the enemy by Queen Catimandua.

This map shows the Roman invasion and the main stages of the conquest of Britain.

✿ Look at the map. Which part of Britain was never conquered by the Romans?

The biggest British revolt came a few years later, in AD 60. King Prasutagus of the Iceni tribe died and the Romans arrogantly seized his lands. Nobles were thrown out of their homes and King Prasutagus's wife, Queen Boudicca, was flogged like a slave. Faced with this outrage the Iceni and their neighbours rose up in a grim rebellion. Led by Boudicca they wiped out the Roman colony at Colchester and burned London.

The Roman governor, Suetonius Paulinus, was caught unawares. He was busy fighting a war in Wales and most of the Roman army was with him. He hurried back to fight the rebels in a desperate battle. About 80,000 Celts were killed and Boudicca poisoned herself rather than being taken prisoner after the defeat.

DETECTIVE WORK

The Roman writer Dio Cassius wrote a description of Boudicca in AD 210. He began: *'She was very tall and terrifying to look at. Her eyes flashed fiercely and her voice was harsh'.* Find the rest of his account on the Internet and draw a portrait of her.

Skulls found in the Walbrook stream in London. Archaeologists think they may have been victims of Boudicca's army.

I was whipped by the Romans when they tried to take our lands – and now I am fighting for my freedom. Think how many of us are fighting and why. We must win this battle or die. Let men live as slaves if they want. I will not.

Boudicca's speech to her army before her last battle. Written in AD 210 by the Roman historian Dio Cassius.

5. Why did the Romans build Hadrian's Wall?

In the years after Claudius, Roman **Emperors** realised that the **Empire** could not go on growing forever. There was a need to mark out the borders and make them safe against attacks from **barbarian** tribes. When the Emperor Hadrian visited Britain in AD 122 he decided to set up a northern frontier. This was to be a mighty wall stretching from the River Tyne in the East to the Solway Firth in the West (see map on page 15).

Hadrian's Wall was largely planned and built by three Roman **legions**, the II, VI and XX. Many of the men were skilled craftsmen such as masons, blacksmiths and carpenters, while some officers were experienced architects and engineers. When they were not fighting, Roman soldiers often worked on big construction projects like forts, **aqueducts** and bridges.

🐾 How good are you at Roman numerals? What are the modern numbers of the legions that built Hadrian's Wall?

When the barbarians had been driven back and Britain had recovered, Hadrian ordered work on a wall which was to be 80 miles long, to divide the Romans from the barbarians.

Roman writer Aelius Spartianus, writing in about AD 390.

Today, Hadrian's Wall is a popular tourist destination. Thousands of people walk the wall every year.

Surveying and building the wall took 12 years. It was 118 kilometres long, 2 to 3 metres high and up to 7 metres wide. Originally painted white to stand out, it snaked across the country, always commanding the high ground. At every mile there was a small fort called a milecastle and in between were two **signal turrets.**

Hadrian's Wall was not meant to stop people travelling in and out of Roman territory, but to control them. If there was an attack, messages could be sent quickly along the wall – or to forts behind – by runners or by **semaphore.** The soldiers who manned the wall were not the legionaries who built it, they were auxiliaries (support troops) from all over the Empire: **Gaul**, Spain, Germany – and as faraway as Syria. Many of them married native girls and settled down in nearby towns. Often their sons served on the Wall after them.

The bath house at Chester's fort. Hadrian's Wall could be a cold and uncomfortable posting for a soldier. A warm bath house would have been a good place to relax.

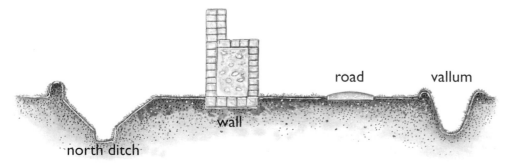

A cross-section of Hadrian's Wall. In front of the wall was a ditch 3 metres deep. Behind was the vallum, a flat bottomed ditch, to keep civilians away.

6. Why did the Romans build roads?

There were no roads as we think of them in Britain before the Romans came. The Celts used ancient tracks some of which were paved, but in wet weather or winter most were impassable. Soon after the invasion, the Roman army began to build a network of brilliantly engineered, all-weather, roads. Using these roads, soldiers could march quickly from fort to fort – or to a trouble spot, such as Hadrian's Wall. Once made, the roads became important for trade with merchants moving their goods from town to town in heavy ox-carts, the goods lorries of the ancient world.

A carving showing an ox-cart. They carried goods like wine, wheat or fine pottery.

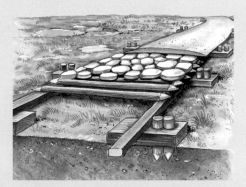

Surveyors came to mark out
The line of the road. After them
Came diggers, packing firm
The trench to stop the road sinking
Or the soil from shifting under the pavement.
Then, the laying of kerbs,
The mating of block with block.

The gangs are busy
Stripping nearby hills of timber,
Making the wooden ties and smoothing in
Lumps of masonry; between each block
Mortar to bind it and fire-dried sand.

Statius, a Roman poet, describing a new road near Rome in about AD 80. The remains of Roman roads in Britain show that the same building methods were used.

A cross-section showing Roman methods of road building on soft and firm ground.

This map shows the most important roads in Britain, about AD 150. Can you find the Fosse Way?

The standard of Roman roads was very high. Firstly, **surveyors** planned the route, then the soldiers set to work. They cut deep drainage ditches on both sides of the line of the road, about 10 metres apart. Next, a foundation of clay, gravel or local stone, like chalk, was laid. Finally, the surface of cement and paving stones was rammed into place with stout timbers. On boggy ground the soldiers laid a framework of timber piles or brushwood to stop the road sinking.

Roman roads were usually very straight. As conquerors they had no need to worry about who owned the land. Unlike today's road planners, they simply went from place to place by the most direct route. Roads built in Britain were part of a wider network of at least 70,000 kilometres of highways knitting the Empire together. A message sent from Rome by the *cursus publicus*, the imperial post, could arrive at Hadrian's Wall in just two weeks. Messengers changed horses every 10 miles and could travel 135 kilometres a day.

❖ What does the map tell us about Roman control of Britain?

DETECTIVE WORK

One of the longest and straightest roads in Britain is the Fosse Way. Use a library encyclopaedia or Internet search to find out about the history of this road. How much of it is still in use and what modern names does it have?

7. What was life like in a Roman town?

The Celts had hill-forts where they would gather in times of danger, but there were no Celtic towns. The Romans, however, believed that civilised life meant town life. To encourage the British to live like Romans they built model towns, such as St Albans and Canterbury, for them to copy. These settlements were based on army forts, with a town wall and neat streets laid out in a grid pattern.

Most Roman towns had the same features. At the main crossroads in the centre was the forum. This was a market square with shops along three sides and the basilica on the fourth. The basilica was the heart of Roman power. This was a large hall where the town council met, people paid their taxes and law courts were held. In serious trials suspects and witnesses could be whipped to make them give information.

This **aerial** photograph shows the remains of the Roman theatre at St Albans in Hertfordshire.

The forum would bustle with shoppers, especially on market days. Roman shops sold many different goods including bread, fish, clothes, shoes, jewellery and weapons.

❧ What do you think the shop in this Roman carving is selling?

It's impossible to get to sleep. You hear heavy wagons creaking through narrow streets and you're deafened by the swearing of cattle drivers whose beasts have got stuck... When you've locked up your house and brought the shutters down on your shop, and the street is still and quiet, there'll always be a burglar to rob you.

Juvenal, the famous Roman poet wrote this comic description of the problems of town life in about AD 120.

Other public buildings made town life lively. Public baths had steam rooms for sweating out dirt from your skin, but they were not just for getting clean. Bathers exercised, talked, played board games and gambled. If people were looking for excitement, the oval shaped amphitheatre was packed every holiday. Eager crowds gathered to watch wild animals fight or **gladiators** pitted against one another. Some towns, like Colchester, had a theatre where plays were put on with music and dancing. Busy inns sold food, wine and local beer while offering weary travellers a place to stable horses and sleep.

Bath houses also had public toilets. There were no cubicles and people sat together in rows, as this postcard shows. They used sponges instead of toilet paper.

Larger towns had facilities we take for granted today. For the first time in Britain, clean water was brought in by a system of **aqueducts** and pipes, while drains and sewers were built to keep streets clean. Even so, many streets were still narrow, smelly and crowded. Ordinary people lived in simple wood-framed houses, sometimes with a shop or workshop at the front. The walls were made from wattle and daub (see page 7) but were often brightly decorated inside, perhaps with flowers or drawings of animals.

DETECTIVE WORK

Try this Roman recipe for stuffed dates, with the help of an adult slave. Remove the stones from the dates and stuff them with anything you like: fruit, nuts, cake crumbs or spices. Roll them in a little salt and fry in honey.

8. What was life like in the Roman countryside?

Although towns were important for encouraging the Celts to live like Romans, only about 250,000 people in Britain (out of a population of 3 million) lived in them. Most British people barely changed their way of life during the centuries of Roman rule. They may have used Roman coins, pots and tools; they may have sold their crops in town markets, but they kept on living in thatched, round houses in small villages and farmsteads.

Some wealthy Britons, however, eagerly copied Roman ideas about farming. They built **villas**, grew new crops and lived a Roman lifestyle. The biggest villas were large and luxurious country houses like Fishbourne, near Chichester, in Sussex. This may have been the palace of Cogidubnus, a Celtic King who became a Roman citizen. Such grand villas were built of stone around a sunlit courtyard. They had central heating, piped water, hot baths, mosaic floors and wall-paintings. The remains of over 600 villas have been found in England.

Every corner is tight packed with corn. Fierce bulls roam in the valleys. The farmyard is full of geese, peacocks and partridges. Home born infant slaves collect the eggs. One farm worker brings in a huge cheese, another a basket of dormice, a third pale honey in its comb.

The Roman writer Varro describes a villa in Italy in the first century BC.

A reconstruction of a Roman villa at Butser Ancient Farm, in Hampshire.

🐾 Look at the quote by Varro. What do you think the Romans did with dormice?

Villas were not just homes, they were the focus of bustling **estates** run to make money. Villas supplied most of the food for the army and people who lived in towns, so usually they were built near a road. To meet this demand, exciting new types of fruit and vegetables were grown for the first time: carrots, parsnips, celery, black plums, cherries, walnuts, apples, pears and even grapes. In fact, many of the foods we know today. Breeds of farm animals too, like pigs, were improved to become bigger and fatter with crops like turnips being grown for fodder to feed the animals over the winter.

Villas were home not only to the landowner and his family, but also their servants and slaves who worked the land. Slaves were the property of their masters and could be kept in chains and beaten. At a villa at Hambleden in Buckinghamshire many bodies of newborn children have been found. Historians think they were left to die – the unwanted babies of slave women.

A recostruction of the inside of a Roman Villa. The corridor is decorated ready for a feast and the mosaic on the wall shows a hunting scene.

9. What gods did the Romans worship?

The Romans did not believe in just one god. They worshipped the many gods made famous by the Greeks, but gave them Roman names. For example, the most powerful Greek god, Zeus, they called Jupiter. When the Romans invaded Britain they brought their beliefs with them and built temples in honour of their gods. A typical Roman town would have temples dedicated to Jupiter, Mars, Minerva, Juno and Mercury.

The Romans believed that success or failure in life depended on the support of the gods and made offerings to gain their favour. An offering might be money, a model of an injured body part, a small statue or the sacrifice of a sheep or goat. Priests looked at the insides of these dead animals for messages from the gods. The shape and colour of a goat's liver, for example, was meant to foretell good or bad news.

Christianity first came to Britain in the fourth century AD. This mosaic floor from a **villa** in Dorset shows a rare portrait of Jesus.

DETECTIVE WORK
Jupiter, Neptune, Mars, Apollo, Mercury, Juno, Minerva, Diana and Venus were all important Roman gods. Find out their Greek names and their powers. Look in your school library for books about the Ancient Greeks. List them in a chart like this:

Roman name	Power	Greek name
Jupiter		

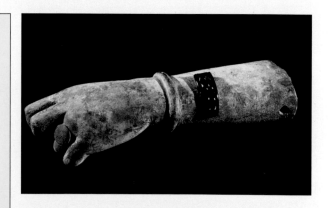

✿ Look at the model of the arm. Why might someone leave this in a temple?

The British worshipped the spirits of nature like the sun, sea, rivers and trees. Usually the Romans treated these foreign gods with great respect – just in case they offended them. At Bath, for example, where hot springs bubbled from the ground, the Britons worshipped a goddess called Sulis. The Romans thought she was similar to their goddess of healing, Minerva, and built a temple in honour of the joint goddess Sulis-Minerva.

Unusually, the Romans were determined to wipe out one feature of British religion, the Druids. The Druids were priests with huge influence in Celtic tribes. Sometimes they sacrificed people in sacred groves, making **prophecies** as they watched their victims die. The Druids had fought the Romans in **Gaul** and led the **resistance** to Roman rule in Britain. The Roman army destroyed the Druid stronghold on the Isle of Anglesey in AD 60, ending Druid power.

To the divine Jupiter, I Vassinus, made a vow before I left home on a journey. I promised to pay six denarii to the gods if they brought me home safely. Thanks to the gods I completed my journey unharmed. This inscription has been set up as proof that I have paid what I owed.

An inscription by a grateful traveller.

Mithras, the Persian god of truth and light, killing a wild bull. The Romans worshipped gods from all over their Empire and Mithras was popular among Roman soldiers serving in Britain. A temple to Mithras was found at Carrawburgh on Hadrian's Wall.

10. What did women do in Roman Britain?

Women in Roman Britain lived in a world run by men. The father was respected as the head of the household. He was the provider who worked hard to support his family and owned all their belongings. Everyone had to obey him.

Girls in richer families rarely married for love. Their fathers chose their husbands for them, often to bring two families together for business or political reasons. Once married, wives were expected to have healthy children and to be good mothers and homemakers. Daily duties included giving orders to the household slaves, sending them to do the shopping and telling them what to cook for the evening dinner party. Only a few better-off women are known to have earned their own living, perhaps as a doctor or painter.

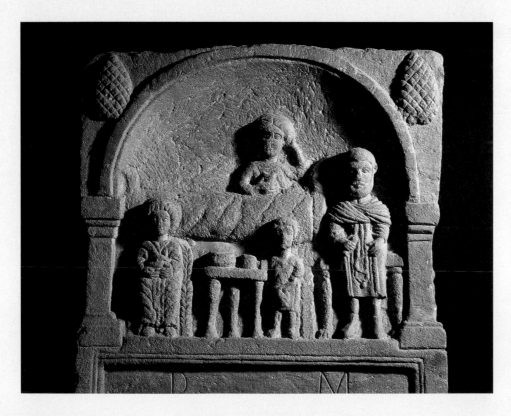

The tombstone of Julia Velva from York.

Roman women often wore their hair in complicated styles held in place by hairpins like this one found in London. The head of the pin shows a woman with just such an elaborate hairstyle.

❀ What does Julia's tombestone tell us about her and her family?

Poorer Roman women could not afford to stay at home, but they did have more freedom. Some worked alongside their husbands in the family shop or on the farm — or they even ran their own business. Others left their children in the care of a neighbour and went out to work. Women's jobs included being an innkeeper, maid, laundress, **seamstress**, actress, musician, nurse or midwife. Wealthy families always had jobs for good nurses and midwives and sometimes they were so highly thought of that they were remembered on family tombs. In 2004, **archaeologists** were astonished to discover the remains of two extraordinary women. They had served as soldiers in a cavalry unit near Hadrian's Wall around AD 220 – 300.

Stranger, my message is short. Stop and read it. This is the unlovely tomb of a lovely woman. Her parents gave her the name Claudia. She loved her husband with all her heart. She bore two children, one whom she left on earth, the other beneath it. She had a pleasing way of talking and walking. She tended the house and worked wool. I have said my piece.

An **epitaph** to Claudia written in about 200 BC, probably by her husband. This give us an idea of how the Romans believed a perfect woman should behave.

Slave women were the unluckiest Roman women. Most slaves were prisoners of war and sold by slave dealers. They became the property of their owners and had to obey their orders, perhaps working in a mine or flour mill where life was hard and short. Only a few were lucky enough to marry their master or save enough money to buy their freedom.

The tombstone of Regina, a Celtic woman who dressed like a Roman. Her husband was Barates, a trader from a city on the edge of the Arabian desert. He bought her as a slave, freed her and made her his wife.

✿ Find the word LIBERTA on Regina's tomb. What do you think this means?

DETECTIVE WORK

Visit your local museum and find out if there are any Roman tombstones. Sketch or photograph the tombstones and make a display. What do they tell you about the Romans who lived in your area?

11. Why did Roman rule in Britain come to an end?

In AD 410, the last Roman soldiers pulled out and the British were left alone to face fierce attacks from Saxon raiders. In AD 446, they wrote a desperate plea for help to the **Emperor**: 'The barbarians drive us into the sea and the sea drives us back to the barbarians… either we are drowned or we are killed.' But no help came. What had happened to the Roman Empire?

Unluckily for the British, the whole Roman Empire was breaking up. In AD 367, the Picts from Scotland had overrun Hadrian's Wall and it took the Romans months to drive them out. But elsewhere far worse trouble was brewing. **Barbarian** tribes like the Goths and Vandals

from the steppes of Central Asia were eager to invade the eastern frontiers. The Vandals made their way through the Empire, attacking the Romans all the way to Spain and on to North Africa. On New Years Eve AD 406–7, the River Rhine froze and German invaders crossed over, taking control of **Gaul** and cutting off Britain from the rest of the Empire. In AD 410, the Goths captured and burned Rome itself.

There seemed to be chaos everywhere. Taxes went up to pay for the huge army needed to fight the invaders. At the same time, long distance trade slowed down, prices went up and industries began to collapse. In Britain, people began to abandon their towns and **villas**.

These silver dishes come from a Roman treasure hoard found at Mildenhall in East Anglia. **Archaeologists** believe the hoard was buried to keep it safe from Saxon pirates.

From AD 340 onwards, Britain became a hotbed of revolt against the emperor in Rome. Again and again ambitious Roman generals, backed by the British, started **civil wars** to seize power in Rome and rule the whole Empire. One of the best known is Magnus Maximus. He was a Spanish soldier who had been sent to Britain to organise the defences but instead he declared himself Emperor and used the **legions** in Britain to take control of Gaul, Spain and Africa for five years. Fighting among themselves like this left the Romans open to attack from their enemies.

A coin showing the head of Magnus Maximus.

*Splendid this fort
  wall is, though fate
  destroyed it.
The city building fell
  apart, the works
Of giants crumbled.
Tumbled are the towers,
Ruined the roofs and
  broken the barred gate,
Frost in the plaster, holes
  in the ceilings,
Torn and collapsed
  by age.*

A poem written in the sixth century by an Anglo-Saxon looking at the remains of Roman Bath.

🐾 Look at the photo of the fort at Porchester. Do you think the whole fort was built by Romans?

This aerial photograph shows the Roman fort at Porchester, near Portsmouth. It was one of a chain of forts built to protect the south and east coasts from raiders.

12. How do we know about the Romans in Britain?

If you wanted to find out about life when your grandparents were children there would be lots for you to look at. Your grandparents could tell you what their lives were like, they might show you family photographs, letters and diaries. You could go to the library to look at newspapers and history books. The local museum might have clothes and toys. All of these things are evidence about the past. When you study the Romans however, the evidence is much harder to find – after all, you are looking back over 2,000 years! But for history detectives there are two main types of evidence to discover – written records and archaeological remains.

Roman pottery tells us a lot about everyday life in Roman times. Sometimes the contents of jars indicate what Romans ate and drank. Sometimes the decorations on the outside of Roman pottery show scenes from Roman life, like this vase found in Colchester.

🐾 What do you think the vase shows?

DETECTIVE WORK

Try burying different things in the ground such as an apple, a ham sandwich, a glass bottle or an animal bone. Dig them up after a few months (make sure you wear some gardening gloves when you do this, as it could be messy!). Write a report on what has happened to them. Which items have **decomposed** the most and why?

The foundations of modern buildings are so deep that they can destroy any evidence of the past. Archaeologists are often called in to study a site before building work begins.

Many Romans could read and write, and some of their work has survived – often because copies were made over the centuries. Written records include fiction such as plays, poetry and poems and factual items such as medical books, histories by Roman historians and even letters from **Emperors**. However, we are limited by what ancient writers chose to record and by their often one-sided point of view. A historian called Suetonius, for example, blamed the Roman invasion of Britain on the British. According to him 'they [the British] kept stirring up trouble'. Worst of all, we know that over the many years since Roman times most of their writing has been lost – by chance, by fires or because it was destroyed on purpose.

Luckily, historians can turn to archaeology to add to the story. **Archaeologists** look at the physical evidence that has survived – often the rubbish the Romans left behind. This includes objects like coins, broken pottery, smashed stone carvings and buildings that have collapsed. Roman sites are often found by taking **aerial** photographs. The outlines of old settlements show as patterns in fields of growing crops.

When the archaeologists start work they have to dig. Most Roman remains are around a metre or more below ground because activities over the centuries, like farming or dumping refuse, have buried them. Some Roman objects survived well, such as those made from baked clay or glass. Others made from **organic material**, like leather shoes or even human bodies, usually decay very quickly and are only preserved in waterlogged soil.

A fantastic source of written evidence has been found at the Roman fort of Vindolanda, near Hadrian's Wall. Hundreds of postcard sized messages written on thin pieces of wood have been preserved in waterlogged soil. The top tablet shown here is a birthday party invitation from Claudia Severa to Sulpicia Lepidina. The handwriting is one of the earliest known examples of writing in Latin by a woman.

13. Your project

Now that it is time to think about your project, you are in for a shock. Did you know that the Romans are still with us today? They are with us because their ideas still influence the way we live. Try a piece of research on our Roman heritage. Here are a few suggestions.

Project Themes and Presentation

Look at the photograph of the Pantheon in Rome, built on the orders of the **Emperor** Hadrian. Roman styles of architecture have been widely copied through the centuries. Are there any buildings near you with features like pillars, arches and pediments? Take photographs and make a PowerPoint presentation.

Our calendar is based on the one worked out by Julius Caesar. Find out which months are named after Roman gods and emperors and write short biographies of them. Use books on the Romans to help you, and look out for chapter headings like 'The Roman Legacy' or 'What did the Romans do for us?'

- The Roman language was Latin. Most modern countries that were part of the Roman **Empire** use many words that come from Latin. Make a dictionary of Latin words and phrases that we use today, for example: status quo = 'things stay the same'.
- Roman ideas about town planning and sanitation still shape the towns we live in now. What facilities did Roman towns have that we still use today? Make an illustrated directory, using your home town as an example.

The Pantheon, in Rome, was built in about AD 125. Features from this building, such as arches and pillars, have been copied all over the world.

Here are a few more ideas:

● Go shopping and look for Latin brand names, like Aero and Flora.
● Compare the design of Roman and modern coins.
● Research how great artists have been influenced by Roman styles of art.

Sherlock Bones has been finding out about hunting dogs from Roman Britain. He found out that they were fast, tough and strong. This meant they were valuable and sold all over the Empire. The Romans liked them so much, that sometimes, they sacrificed them to the gods – or put them in arenas to fight lions or bears. Today's wolfhounds and mastiffs are their descendants.

Roman hunting dogs looked like this modern wolfhound.

Glossary

AD The years after Christ's birth.

aerial photograph A photo taken from a plane. This is one of the best ways for archaeologists to spot evidence of Roman buildings.

ally A friend.

aqueducts Raised channels, sometimes as big as bridges, carrying water over long distances.

archaeologists People who study remains from ancient times.

barbarians A Roman word for uncivilised people.

BC The years before Christ's birth.

civil wars Wars between people in the same country, not against outside enemies.

conquered To be defeated and taken over.

decompose To rot away.

emperor The ruler of an empire. The first Roman Emperor was called Augustus.

empire A country or state which rules over a number of other countries.

epitaph Words carved on a tomb.

estates Large farms.

Gaul The Roman province that covered France, Belgium and the Rhine region of Germany.

gladiators A specially trained warrior fighting to entertain the crowds. Sometimes they fought to the death.

hostages Prisoners who are held to guarantee the good behaviour of their people.

Iceni A tribe in East Anglia.

legion A Roman army unit with about 5,500 men.

merchants People who made a living by buying and selling things.

organic material Items that are made from things that were once alive, like leather from cattle skin.

prophecy To tell the future.

resistance A group of people who wanted to throw the Romans out of power.

seamstress A woman who makes a living by sewing.

semaphore A system of sending messages by flags or flashes of light from lanterns.

signal turret A watch tower.

standard bearer The soldier who carried the sacred symbol of the legion: an eagle on a pole.

surveyors A person who planned engineering projects, like the route of a road.

villa A country house.

Further Information

Books to read
Britain in Roman Times by Tim Locke (Franklin Watts, 2008)

The Romans: Reconstructed by Jason Hook (Wayland, 2007)

On the Trail of the Romans in Britain by Richard Wood (Franklin Watts, 2000)

Men, Women and Children in Ancient Rome by Jane Bingham (Wayland, 2007)

Websites
Take a look at the Museum of Antiquities website:
http://museums.ncl.ac.uk/archive/index.html

Take an interactive tour of Roman Colchester at:
www.colchestermuseums.org.uk

The Romans in Britain is a huge website packed with information. Go on line at:
www.romans-in-britain.org.uk

Answers

Places to visit

Hadrian's Wall has many places to visit. Two of the best are Segedunum Fort at Wallsend near Newcastle and Housesteads Fort, six miles from Haltwhistle.

Visit the reconstructed Roman villa and Iron Age farm at Butser Ancient Farm near Petersfield, Hampshire. (www.butser.org.uk)

See the remains of brilliant first century mosaics at Fishbourne Roman Palace Chichester, West Sussex. (www.sussexpast.co.uk/fishbourne/)

Many museums have excellent Roman finds. A good one is Verulamium Museum, St Albans, Hertfordshire. (www.stalbansmuseums.org.uk)

Page 5 ❧ Games such as fights between gladiators or wild animals.

Page 7 ❧ Three sets of walls. If attackers broke through one set they would face an even higher set of walls in front of them.

Page 8 ❧ To make his victories over the British seem all the greater. As if to say 'look at all the problems my army faced, but I still won'.

Page 10 ❧ Northern Scotland.

Page 12 ❧ The Second, Sixth and Twentieth.

Page 15 ❧ There are few roads in Wales and Scotland, showing the Romans never fully controlled them.

Page 16 ❧ This shows a butcher cutting a joint of meat. Other cuts of meat are hanging from the ceiling.

Page 18 ❧ They ate them. Stuffed dormice were a Roman delicacy.

Page 20 ❧ To say thank you to the gods when their injured arm healed. Sometimes models were left when someone was still sick to remind the god which body part to heal.

Page 22 ❧ She is lying on a couch surrounded by her family. She is drinking from a cup and there is food on the small table in front of her. These features show she is from a wealthy family.

Page 23 ❧ Liberta means a freed slave – she was given her liberty.

Page 25 ❧ The castle and church were built in the Middle Ages. The walls are Roman. Why let a perfectly good set of Roman walls go to waste?

Page 26 ❧ The vase shows a chariot race.

Index